SCOTT BESSENT

The Visionary Investor

Frank S. Diaz

Scott Bessent

Copyright ©Frank S. Diaz. 2024

All rights reserved. No part of this publication may be reproduced, distributed, or transmitted in any form or by any means, including photocopying, recording, or other electronic or mechanical methods, without the prior written permission of the publisher, except in the case of brief quotations embodied in critical reviews and certain other noncommercial uses permitted by copyright law.

Scott Bessent

TABLE OF CONTENTS

INTRODUCTION

CHAPTER 1: WHO IS SCOTT BESSENT?
- Early Influences And Education
- The Road To Financial Mastery

CHAPTER 2: EARLY CAREER HIGHLIGHTS
- Building Credibility In The Financial World

CHAPTER 3: LESSONS FROM JULIAN ROBERTSON
- Transforming Challenges Into Opportunities

CHAPTER 4: THE LEAP TO INDEPENDENCE

Scott Bessent

    Developing A Visionary Strategy

CHAPTER 5: UNDERSTANDING MARKETS: LOCAL AND GLOBAL

    Risk Management And Adaptive Thinking

CHAPTER 6: KEY INVESTMENTS THAT SHAPED HIS CAREER

    Analyzing The Traits Of A Visionary

CHAPTER 7: CONTRIBUTIONS TO THE FINANCIAL INDUSTRY

    Passing The Torch Of Innovation

    Scott's Influence On International Market

CONCLUSION

INTRODUCTION

Scott Bessent is a visionary whose ideas have transformed the financial landscape in ways few could have predicted, not merely an investor.

From his early days as a rising star on Wall Street to his presidency of George Soros's financial empire and the founding of his billion-dollar hedge fund, Key Square Group, Bessent's career is a masterclass in foresight, flexibility, and intelligence.

In Scott Bessent: The Visionary Investor, you will reach the head of a financial genius who has regularly exceeded market trends and changed what it means to think about significant investing. From negotiating economic crises to

Scott Bessent

making audacious wagers that paid off brilliantly, this book looks at the pivotal events that shaped his career.

It explores the ideas, techniques, and personal attributes that have set Bessent apart in the cutthroat realm of hedge funds.

But this is about the human spirit underlying the deals, not only about statistics and markets. Bessent's narrative is one of bravery, inquiry, and relentless inventiveness.

Whether you are interested in high-stakes finance, a seasoned expert, or just someone interested, this book provides insightful analysis from one of the most influential personalities in contemporary investing.

Scott Bessent

The fantastic narrative of Scott Bessent, a real visionary who has converted risk into opportunity and changed the financial industry, will inspire, challenge, and enthral you.

CHAPTER 1: WHO IS SCOTT BESSENT?

In the financial industry, Scott Bessent is a name connected with genius. He is a maverick investor whose career unfolds like an exciting story of intuition, creativity, and big wagers.

From the high-stakes trading desks of Wall Street to guiding one of the most significant hedge funds in history, Bessent has created a legacy marked by his remarkable ability to identify possibilities where others see turmoil.

But Scott Bessent goes beyond headlines and billion-dollar portfolios. Once stunning George Soros with his keen observations, he became the principal investment officer at Soros Fund Management throughout some of the most turbulent years in economic history. He is the brains behind Key Square Group. This hedge fund rapidly acquired billions of assets and became a financial genius.

Still, his narrative is about the man who views investing like an art form, not about figures or market outsmarting ability. Bessent's skill combines a thorough knowledge of human behaviour with detailed research to see trends others overlook and keep one step ahead of world events.

Apart from the business world, Bessent is a mentor to upcoming talents, a curious mind with an insatiable desire for information, and an eager investigator of what lies ahead. Because of his humour, charisma, and honest observations, he is as fascinating as the markets he negotiates.

Scott Bessent is more than simply an investor; he's a storyteller, a trailblazer, and evidence that, given vision and bravery, it is possible to rewrite the rules of success in finance, and life. For everyone brave enough to dream large, his path inspires respect and possibilities.

Early Influences And Education

Before Scott Bessent started walking Wall Street, he began his path toward visionary investing. Bessent's early years were moulded by academic curiosity and a passion for the surroundings; he was born with a curious mind and a natural ability to detect patterns. Growing up in a family that valued education and discovery, he was drawn to unconventional thinking and problem-solving, qualities that would eventually define his work.

His academic route was also somewhat unusual. Attending Yale University, Bessent concentrated on economics, setting the foundation for his career in finance. However, his Yale experience went beyond textbooks and lectures.

Here, he started developing his critical thinking, questioning conventions, and global viewpoint, qualities that would distinguish him as a leader in the financial industry.

From his early years, Bessent displayed the traits of a contrarian thinker. He wanted to avoid following the herd or taking accepted knowledge at face value. Instead, he aimed to uncover the "why" underlying events and patterns, a practice that would eventually help him become a powerful market movement predictor.

From Yale's classrooms to the early professional mentorships and events, Scott Bessent's early years were a masterclass in preparation. They exposed the seeds of the visionary investor he would become and set the groundwork for his explosive climb in the financial sector.

The Road To Financial Mastery

For Scott Bessent, the road to financial mastery was an exciting trip consisting of abrupt twists, unanticipated detours, and moments of pure genius, not a straight-line path. From his early

Scott Bessent

excursions into Wall Street to running billion-dollar hedge fund empires, Bessent's path was driven by a unique combination of talent, tenacity, and a readiness to welcome danger.

Beginning his work at Brown Brothers Harriman, Bessent jumped headfirst into the hectic world of finance upon Yale graduation. Industry behemoths soon noticed his extraordinary analytical abilities and capacity to plan many steps.

One of the turning points was when he started working closely with the venerable George Soros at Soros Fund Management. This was more than simply a job; it was a tutorial in a high-stakes investment where Bessent learned ideas that would define his attitude to markets.

Scott Bessent

Bessent was naturally adept at detecting trends and opportunities. He could translate ideas into profitable, practical investments, whether negotiating difficult macroeconomic situations or developing plans that defied received wisdom.

After spending time with Soros, he became Chief Investment Officer. He oversaw billion-dollar transactions while guiding the fund through some of its most challenging times.

But Bessent's aspiration did not stop there. In 2015, he started Key Square Group, his hedge fund, and soon, it was among the most profitable and well-known in the business.

Through his firm, Bessent displayed financial acumen and leadership, promoting a culture of innovation and strict thinking consistent with his worldview.

Bessent's journey to mastery was about conquering himself, his instincts, discipline, and capacity to adapt in a constantly changing world, not about figures or market trends. Today, he shows what is possible when vision meets skill and strenuous effort meets opportunity.

CHAPTER 2: EARLY CAREER HIGHLIGHTS

Early in his career, Scott Bessent reads like the ideal precursor to a Wall Street movie, full of ambition, mystery, and a fantastic sense of timing.

Following his 1984 Yale University graduation, Scott focused on the financial industry, where the high-stakes investing game was already humming with possibility.

Starting his path at Brown Brothers Harriman, a prestigious establishment with old-world elegance but not mainly known for risk-taking, Scott was not meant to be a conservative player.

Early on, he showed a natural ability to spot trends others couldn't and to pose concerns nobody else would have considered. Mentors who saw in him the seeds of a future investment genius were drawn to this bright mind.

Run by the renowned short-seller Jim Chanos, the venerable investing company Kynikos Associates marked the next significant chapter.

Scott sharpened his analytical skills at Kynikos, learning to spot overpriced assets that would finally collapse under the weight of their buzz. This job improved his abilities and let him experience the seductive excitement of contrarian investing, betting against the crowd and being right.

However, Scott's actual star-making moment came when he joined the Soros Management Fund in the early 1990s, directly under the most legendary investor of all time, George Soros. Here, Scott's skills came to shine.

Soros's acute mind and worldwide viewpoint perfectly fit his high-octane, global macro approach. The encounter changed him by introducing him to the complexity of world finance and the dizzying speed of decision-making demanded at the top.

Scott was a fundat asset at Soros's fund because of his ability to analyze markets and spot possibilities even in turmoil. His time there prepared him as a superb investor and a strategist with nearly perfect clarity to see around financial corners, laying the groundwork for a fantastic career.

Those early years were about laying the groundwork for a legacy that would rock the investing scene, not only about chewing his teeth.

Scott Bessent was quietly threading a yarn that would make him a financial powerhouse, not merely learning the trade-offs. Scott was more than ready to respond as the future called.

Building Credibility In The Financial World

Scott Bessent's path in the financial industry is simply a masterpiece in strategic thinking, flexibility, and trust-building. His ascent to popularity resulted from keen insights, audacious choices, and relentless credibility building rather than instant success.

Bessent's career is based on a natural ability to strike a mix of brilliance and humility. He developed relationships, not only pursuing profits. During some of the most critical events in world finance, Bessent led as George Soros's former Chief Investment Officer for his Soros Fund Management. Strategic thinking enabled Soros Fund to profit billions, establishing his reputation as a financial wizard.

But Bessent's reputation developed from more than simply numbers. That was his capacity to keep ahead of the curve. He was adept at seeing possibilities before they were clear to others. His choices were ahead of their time, whether related to macroeconomic trends or using data-driven insights. This foresight resulted from careful study and a thorough awareness of market dynamics, not from chance.

Bessent is unique in part because of his sincerity. He didn't establish his reputation by flitting about or being overconfident. Instead, his integrity and consideration grew to define him.

People trusted him for his character and his financial sense of direction. In a field where mistrust is rife, Bessent stood out with his direct attitude.

Another evidence of his confidence and reputation came from his choice in 2015 to leave the Soros Fund and launch Key Square Group, his own company. The change was smooth, and his new business drew billions in capital initially. Investors see a leader who routinely produces returns without sacrificing ethics, not only a fund manager.

The tale of Scott Bessent reminds us that in the financial sector, credibility is more about connections than returns. It's about being creative but grounded, audacious but controlled.

His legacy reminds us that success is about being the one everyone believes will make the correct decision, not only about being the most intelligent person in the room. In a business as competitive as finance trust is the ultimate currency, too.

CHAPTER 3: LESSONS FROM JULIAN ROBERTSON

Renowned investor and Key Square Group founder Scott Bessent spent his early years under the direction of Tiger Management's venerable hedge fund manager, Julian Robertson.

The lessons he learned from Robertson are as fascinating as they are instructive; they combine humour, energy, and genius, moulding Bessent's career and inspiring investors worldwide.

Picture entering a room with Julian Robertson. You will likely find him pacing, passionately analyzing a market trend, or contesting the belief of a new analyst. For Scott Bessent, it was like walking into a pressure cooker of knowledge, passion, and occasionally pure fear.

Robertson's unrelenting pursuit of perfection was a curse as much as a gift. It challenged Bessent to his limits and let him realize that investing is a struggle of wits, tenacity, and a little audacity, not only about statistics.

Among the important lessons was the value of conviction. Robertson pounded into his protégés that "kinda sure" was insufficient. When your gut and studies indicated an opportunity, you had to have the bravery to gamble large.

Bessent remembers how this idea was lived, not merely a theory. Robertson expected his squad to be daring, as he was not hesitant about making such moves. Bessent once observed how a thorough investigation of a firm could result in an overnight multi-million dollar position. But conviction also carried responsibility, you owned it if you made a mistake.

Still, another unforgettable lecture was on the art of hiring. Robertson was naturally gifted, but he also coached Bessent on the value of surrounding herself with people who push her.

Mediocrity was not an option; Robertson thought of creating groups of intelligent, opinionated people capable of maintaining their position in a discussion. For Bessent, this meant having explosive conversations and rising massively as an investor.

Robertson's passion for contrarian ideas may be one of the most interesting revelations. Should the market be headed one way, his natural inclination was to give the opposite side at least some thought.

This was a systematic search for hidden value, not only disobedience for its own sake. Bessent learnt to welcome the discomfort of bucking the herd, even when it felt like swimming upstream in a sea of naysayers.

At last, there was the resilience lesson. Making investments in Tiger Management was not for the timid. Errors were public and frequently embarrassing, not just teaching opportunities.

Still, Robertson advised Bessent that the secret was not to avoid failing but to bounce back better. The markets would humble you, but the test was how fast you could get back on your feet and onward.

Scott Bessent sometimes characterizes his time at Tiger as a transforming event, combining a gladiator arena, boot camp, and chess match.

Working with Julian Robertson was about building the mental toughness to survive in a world that hardly displays kindness, not only about learning how to invest.

For those lucky enough to hear Bessent tell these tales, it is abundantly evident that Robertson's teachings are ageless and equally exciting as the man himself.

Scott Bessent

Transforming Challenges Into Opportunities

In the financial realm, Scott Bessent is a name connected with creativity, strategy, and grit. Renowned for his keen intellect and unwavering will, he has created a career akin to an exciting journey.

From the trade floor to international investment strategy conferences, Bessent has repeatedly shown that obstacles are only chances in disguise.

His story is interesting not only because of his outstanding credentials but also because of his different thinking approach. Many view risk when confronted with erratic markets or changing economic trends; Bessent sees promise.

He lives on change, not only adapts to it. His talent for converting challenges into stepping stones has helped to establish him as a financial maverick.

One of Bessent's career highlights is his tenure as Chief Investment Officer atoros Fund Management. Imagine being given billions of dollars to oversee under the wary eye of great investor George Soros. Most would find this to be an impossible task.

For Bessent, it was an opportunity for brilliance. He not only preserved the tradition of the fund but also drove it to unprecedented heights with creative ideas and audacious choices during his tenure.

Once he left Soros, he never rested on his laurels. Instead, he opened Key Square Group, his hedge fund. Like a chess player, the name suggests his strategic mind, constantly several moves ahead.

Key Square rapidly grew among history's most significant hedge fund introductions, evidence of Bessent's standing and imaginative ideas.

Beyond the board room, Bessent distinguishes himself by his intellectual curiosity. He is passionate about understanding the forces shaping the planet, from geopolitical dynamics to technological developments.

Scott Bessent

This all-encompassing viewpoint helps him negotiate the intricate network of world markets with assurance and insight.

Still, it's more than just strategy and spreadsheets. Bessent is as engaging in person as in interviews; he is renowned for his humour and friendliness.

He has a way of making even the most difficult subjects enjoyable, whether offering observations on the direction of finance or relating stories from his career.

In the always-shifting terrain of finance, where unpredictability is the only constant, Scott Bessent is a lighthouse of flexibility and inventiveness. His path is a master class in spotting chances where others might view dead

Scott Bessent

ends. His narrative teaches us just one thing: the best benefits often result from boldly, curiously, and with courage facing the most challenging obstacles.

CHAPTER 4: THE LEAP TO INDEPENDENCE

In global finance, Scott Bessent's rise to independence is a story of vision, tenacity, and financial brilliance that reads like a fascinating adventure.

Imagine a seasoned investor with a remarkable ability to see around corners, leaving a profitable position to forge his path in the high-stakes hedge fund space. That's the core of Bessent's audacious decision to start Key Square Group in 2015.

Bessent was most famously the Chief Investment Officer for Soros Fund Management before this jump. Indeed, Soros is the man who famously "broke the Bank of England." Bessent developed his skills under Soros's tutoring, learning the complex dance of macro investing.

He has accomplished excellent results and helped oversee about $30 billion by 2015. Still, he opted to jump right in and launch his own company instead of lounging about his credentials.

Why would one leave a position this sought-after? It went beyond just financial considerations. Independence for Bessent meant freedom: the capacity to carry out his ideas, take calculated chances on his terms, and produce something especially his. Key Square Group's founding was a statement of personal ambition and inventiveness rather than only a business one.

The sheer scope of his debut made his story enjoyable. Unlike many first-time hedge fund founders who start small, Bessent raised an impressive $2 billion for Key Square right from the beginning.

That degree of investor confidence revealed much about his reputation and ability. He created a financial behemoth intended to flourish in the complex, constantly changing global economy, not only a hedge fund.

But Bessent was broader in scope than spreadsheets and numbers. He was renowned for his intellectual curiosity and varied interests, which gave the financial industry a unique flair.

He was a creative thinker and artist, traits that often translated into audacious, unusual investing ideas.

His independence also represented a more significant change in the financial sector when more elite investors sought to veer from established companies to create their routes. Bessent's narrative became a lighthouse for people hoping to seize control of their lives in a cutthroat sector.

Of course, the path to freedom presented difficulties. Negotiating the world markets is like riding a rollercoaster blindfolded; one mistake can cost millions. But Bessent proved he was not merely a follower in Soros's footsteps but a trailblazer in his own right by balancing caution with conviction and taking measured risks.

Scott Bessent

The path of Scott Bessent is an inspirational tale about ambition, bravery, and the craft of reinventions, not only a finance one. It is evidence that occasionally, you must leap if you are to fly.

Developing A Visionary Strategy

In the field of visionary strategy, Scott Bessent's name calls attention. His method is about seeing a future before it ever occurs, not only about following the newest trends or numbing calculations.

He is like a financial fortune teller, but instead of crystal balls, he employs thorough research, creative thinking, and an unquestionable belief in the ability of strategy to change companies.

Scott Bessent

Bessent is the kind of leader dissatisfied with the current quo. He sees possibilities disguised as obstacles ready to be untangled. Whether in the financial markets or leadership circles, his career has been a master class in negotiating unknown terrain.

His capacity to look beyond the usual distinguishes him. Often years ahead of his rivals, he is already orienting his businesses and himself for the future rather than merely reacting to the present.

Developing a visionary plan for Bessent is a journey rather than a one-time occurrence. He thinks about creating plans that change with the times and might bend and stretch without breaking.

This implies thinking big and ahead, contemplating the long game, and how each choice now influences tomorrow's larger picture. It's about remaining flexible and agile and constantly feeling the pulse of what's ahead.

One of the most impressive features of his strategy is his almost perfect foresight of changing market conditions. Bessent is already headed for the next great opportunity, while others are flitting about reacting to changes.

This foresight is a mix of experience, thorough knowledge of market patterns, and a natural sense of what the future holds, not magic.

Not all of it, though, is about mind reading. Visionary plans centre on producing something that endures. Bessent's approach builds foundations for long-term success rather than merely yielding temporary gains. Resilience is the foundation of his approaches to survive political upheavals, economic crises, and even unanticipated world occurrences.

He stays a modest student of the game through all this; he continuously learns, adapts, and is never too proud to change when needed. This adaptability is essential in a society that is accelerating faster than ever.

In Bessent's perspective, visionary strategy is about foreseeing and influencing the future in significant, sustainable, and transforming ways.

Scott Bessent's path proves that the most excellent way to lead in the future is by considering it now and acting boldly to help shape it. Bessent's approach to visionary strategy provides a lighthouse of clarity, purpose, and relentless determination in a world that sometimes feels spiraling out of control. That is also the true secret of success.

CHAPTER 5: UNDERSTANDING MARKETS: LOCAL AND GLOBAL

Knowing local or international markets is like untying an excellent, constantly shifting narrative. It concerns people, cultures, trends, and the unseen threads linking them, not just numbers and graphs.

Every market has a different rhythm; learning to master it requires both a telescope for worldwide trends and a magnifying glass for local subtleties.

Scott Bessent

It starts right in local markets. Driven by local likes, habits, and customs, they are the beating core of communities. In a local market, one considers why People want what they do, not only what they desire.

Gaining knowledge of these dynamics means living among the residents' daily lives. What values do they hold? Their time and money spent? Relationships and trust are frequently the foundation of local markets. Hence, companies who know this can establish close ties with their target market.

However, local markets are close and specialized yet do not exist in a bubble. Now, we are entering the worldwide market, that large, linked web spanning nations and continents. Here is where trends start, where economies mix, and where chances could show up and disappear in the space of a few seconds. Everything from international trade policies and currency swings to technological developments and geopolitical events shapes global markets.

The difficulty and chance lie in connecting the local and global markets. Unless tailored to fit the regional setting, a product that excels in one area may fail in another. Look at world behemoths like McDonald's or Coca-Cola.

Their success comes from their ability to adapt products to fit local tastes, from McSpicy Paneer burgers in India to green tea-flavoured Coke in Japan, not alone from their worldwide presence.

Technology has made learning these sectors both simpler and more complex. Data and analytics, on the one hand, offer remarkable insights into consumer behaviour that enable companies to forecast trends and hone their plans. Conversely, the rate of change is dizzying. Markets change quickly; being relevant calls for ongoing education and adaptability.

Understanding markets is beautiful because it is as much an art as a science. It's about listening, not only to what consumers are saying but also to what they are not saying, reading signals and seeing patterns. It's about curiosity, open-mindedness, and risk-taking willingness.

Whether negotiating the incredible complexity of a worldwide market or the vivid turmoil of a local market, the secret is to remain grounded and view the future. After all, markets are active, breathing ecosystems. Your ability to serve them, and perhaps even mold them, improves with increasing knowledge.

Risk Management And Adaptive Thinking

The way Scott Bessent approaches adaptive thinking and risk management is like watching a brilliant chess player perform. Every action is organized, planned, and done with the endgame in mind, but with one crucial twist: he knows the board can turn at any moment.

Bessent's approach is beautiful; he is ready for the unexpected and thrives in ambiguity.

In his universe, risk management is not about totally avoiding danger. That would be like attempting boat sailing without ever leaving the harbour. Instead, it's about knowing which hazards are worth risking and which ones to avoid. Risk for Bessent is more of a mystery waiting to be solved than a four-letter term.

However, big rewards accompany enormous risks if you approach them with clarity, preparedness, and a reasonable measure of humility.

His talent for perceiving risk as an opportunity rather than a threat distinguishes him. He expects the unfamiliar, not merely responds to it. Because of his proactive approach, he can make audacious judgments others might avoid.

Always one step ahead of the curve, he is the leader who sees promise where others see danger.

The secret weapon for negotiating the erratic waves of risk is adaptive thinking. Markets are famously erratic; hence, what works now could implode tomorrow. Bessent is a master of adaptability; he does not follow a set agenda.

Should the market shift unexpectedly, he is not just ready to adjust but already in motion. This flexibility on demand is not only a talent but also a mindset. It calls for staying educated, using critical thinking, and being cool under duress.

Bessent's method is among the more interesting ones since he stresses learning. Whether or not a risk pays off, everyone teaches something.

Scott Bessent

Of course, successes are celebrated; however, mistakes are not thrown under the brush; instead, they are analyzed, understood, and used as fuel for better decisions in the future. His growth-oriented approach helps him stay ahead of the game and always invent.

But never let yourself believe that his approaches are all work and no play. Bessent is adept at including imagination and inquiry in his techniques.

He quickly investigates unusual ideas or tests hypotheses that initially look ridiculous. His method is fascinating and successful partly because of his openness to welcoming the unexpected and thinking beyond the box.

Scott Bessent

The perspective of Scott Bessent reminds us that life and business naturally involve risk. It's something to grasp, welcome, and apply to your benefit rather than something to panic over. Using adaptive thinking as his compass, he is changing the game, one measured risk at a time, not just surviving it.

CHAPTER 6: KEY INVESTMENTS THAT SHAPED HIS CAREER

Scott Bessent's career is a display of audacious, transforming investments that determined his path and had a long-lasting effect on the financial industry.

Bessent, who is renowned for his keen sense of direction and open-book reading of the markets, has always been one step ahead, spotting opportunities others either overlooked or discounted. Each one is a masterpiece in planning, timing, and conviction; his significant investments are the stuff of folklore.

Scott Bessent

Managing the legendary Quantum Fund with George Soros gave Bessent one of the turning points in his career. Bessent was important in Soros's now-famous wager against the British pound during the 1992 currency crisis.

Dubbed "Black Wednesday," this audacious short on the pound brought in billions, establishing Soros's reputation as "the man who broke the Bank of England" and securing Bessent's prominence in international banking. This move embodied Bessent's investing philosophy, which combined macroeconomic foresight with exact execution.

Later, Bessent kept proving his mettle while Chief Investment Officer at Soros Fund Management. His calculated wagers on commodities, currencies, and emerging markets drove the fund to breathtakingly high performance. Not one to run from complexity, he frequently sought out underestimated prospects to turn contrarian views into large rewards. Whether negotiating erratic political terrain or predicting changes in world monetary policy, Bessent regularly showed his remarkable ability to keep ahead of the curve.

After starting Key Square Group, his investment company, one of his most interesting career chapters unfolded. Here, Bessent focused primarily on his ideas of long-term thinking and controlled risk-taking.

Key Square gained recognition for its focus on macroeconomic trends and capacity to appraise markets others considered too erratic. While Bessent's emphasis on alternative assets

suggested his readiness to innovate in a constantly shifting financial environment, his investments in Asia and other emerging countries highlighted his global view.
More than just figures on a spreadsheet, Bessent's significant investments represent his capacity to spot trends where others find anarchy.

Whether he is betting on commodities, stocks, or currencies, his choices usually reflect a strong awareness of market dynamics and human behaviour. He forecasts trends, often rewriting the story, not only following them.

Scott Bessent is unique, mostly in his relentless dedication to study and development. Every investment, successful or not, has been a stepping stone contributing to his great reservoir of knowledge and honing his edge. His career is evidence of the ability of vision, flexibility, and bravery to take chances when the consequences are significant.

For those who follow his path, Bessent's investments teach them to negotiate erratic situations, grab possibilities, and translate audacious ideas into innovative reality, not only financial successes. His narrative reminds us that outstanding investors help to shape rather than merely follow the markets.

Analyzing The Traits Of A Visionary

Examining the qualities of a visionary is like breaking out the DNA of someone who can see past the horizon when most of us are staring toward the road ahead. Visionaries shape the future; they do not only forecast it. They question conventions, change the rules, and sometimes leave the planet wondering how they knew what was ahead. But what drives a vision forward? Let us explore the qualities that distinguish these remarkable brains.

Visionaries are, first and most importantly, dreamers, yet they are action-oriented rather than daydreamers. They find opportunities where others might see obstacles.

To them, every challenge is only a riddle waiting to be figured out. Visionaries are driven by an unquestionable belief that the impossible is just a suggestion, whether a ground-breaking idea, a disruptive business strategy, or a revolutionary invention.

Although their playground is imagination, strategy is their toolkit. Visionaries are strategic strategists who know how to realize ideas, not merely creative thinkers.

Drawing lessons from many disciplines and experiences, they can connect unconnected dots. Their capacity to integrate data and approach problems holistically helps them stay ahead of the curve.

Still, another defining quality is resiliency. Visionaries may encounter doubt, criticism, and even failure. Rather than allowing these obstacles to stop them, they feed them.

They pursue nonstop, adjusting and recalibrating as needed. Their resilience goes beyond recovery, including bouncing ahead and becoming more muscular and wiser.

Masters of communication are also visionaries. They are remarkably able to motivate and unite others around their concepts. Their enthusiasm and commitment are contagious for a team, a business, or a whole sector. They can create a vivid picture of the future that others would find impossible to ignore.

Still another underappreciated but vital quality is empathy. Visionaries have a natural sense of people's needs, especially in cases where such needs still need to be clearly expressed.

From the end user's point of view, they foresee challenges and answers, creating almost perfect inventions for their market.

Their faithful friend is curious. Visionaries are lifetime students who never stop asking questions, investigating, and learning new things.

They are not hesitant to question presumptions, including their own. Because of their excellent natural curiosity, their ideas remain fresh and their viewpoints sharp.

Finally, visionaries interact especially with danger. Though they are not irresponsible, they feel good venturing into the future.

Risk to them is not something to be afraid of; instead, it is a required component of development and creativity. They are aware that often playing things safe results in lost chances for personal growth.

Scott Bessent

Ultimately, visionaries combine imagination, bravery, and a dogged ambition to make the world better, or at least different. They are the dreamers who dare, the thinkers who act, and the leaders who motivate others. They help us realize that we make the future; it does not occur to us.

CHAPTER 7: CONTRIBUTIONS TO THE FINANCIAL INDUSTRY

Like his career, Scott Bessent's contributions to the financial sector are audacious and powerful. Bessent has been instrumental in forming modern finance with his creative ideas, keen market analysis, and fearless attitude to risk and opportunity. Over decades, geographies, and asset classes, his impact is felt in the business everywhere.

Among Bessent's most significant accomplishments is his direction throughout the Golden Age of Soros Fund Management. He proved the continuing significance of macroeconomic research. As chief investment officer, he helped one of the most successful hedge funds in the world negotiate difficult times. Fund managers started looking at his capacity to predict market changes and respond quickly.

Bessent's work on the famous short of the British pound during the 1992 currency crisis with George Soros is a pillar of financial history. Although Soros was the public face of the trade, Bessent's behind-the-scenes knowledge was crucial in developing the plan that finally "broke the Bank of England."

This action underlined the influence of macro hedge funds and the need to know the interaction among politics, economy, and market behaviour.

Scott Bessent

After starting Key Square Group, Bessent adopted different approaches and concentrated on long-term, worldwide macroeconomic patterns, offering a novel viewpoint to the sector.

Reflecting Bessent's reputation and inventive ideas, Key Square rapidly became one of history's biggest hedge fund launches. His company became a lighthouse for those looking for consistency and foresight in an increasingly erratic world.

Emphasizing the need to shift with the market dynamics, Bessent has also been a strong champion of flexibility in finance. He has helped the sector enter the twenty-first century by combining new technologies and data-driven insights with classic macro investing.

Scott Bessent

Fund managers struggling with fast technology developments and changing global paradigms find a road map in their forward-looking strategy.

Another noteworthy gift is his dedication to training the next generation of financial executives. Bessent has been immensely helpful in developing talent, imparting knowledge, and advocating the need for intellectual curiosity and grit. His mentoring has shaped some of the most brilliant financial brains, so his influence goes beyond his investments.

Beyond his career successes, Bessent has helped the financial sector through thought leadership. His opinions on risk management, macroeconomic trends, and global markets are much sought after, often impacting more general debates on economic policy and investment strategies.

Scott Bessent's contributions to the financial sector change the game rather than only the numbers. Combining daring bets with rigorous planning, agility with conviction, and invention with a great respect for the basics, he has reinvented what it means to be a macro investor. His legacy is evidence of the need for vision, discipline, and the unrelenting quest for greatness in finance.

Passing The Torch Of Innovation

Regarding passing the innovative flame, Scott Bessent plays the dual roles of mentor and trailblazer. His career is a master class in how to inspire and empower the next generation of financial leaders, not only a tale of personal accomplishment. Innovation for Bessent is a heritage to be cultivated, polished, and passed on, not only a tool for success.

Curiosity and adaptability define Bessent's approach to invention; these traits he actively encourages in everyone around him. According to him, the financial world is constantly changing, and yesterday's plans cannot be applied tomorrow.

Encouragement of his mentees to challenge conventions and welcome change helps them to develop a lifetime of learning and discovery. This philosophy guarantees that innovation is not only a catchphrase but also a live, breathing component of the direction of the sector.

Scott Bessent

Bessent's ideas have always revolved mostly around mentoring. He enjoys guiding talent and has a natural ability to see it. Whether guiding analysts at his company or sharing ideas with colleagues, Bessent imparts critical thinking, bold action, and measured risk-taking skills to others.

He teaches how to think, not only what to do. This difference is vital in a field where adaptation might be the difference between success and failure.

Another way Bessent passes the batons is by advocating cooperation above rivalry. Although the banking sector sometimes seems to be a zero-sum game, he understands that ideas flourish in settings where they are exchanged and polished. He fosters innovative ideas and solutions by building teams that appreciate several points of view. His companies have constantly pushed limits and shown extraordinary success, primarily because of his conviction in collective intelligence.

But Bessent's influence goes beyond his close network. His work has shaped how the whole sector views risk, strategy, and global macroeconomics. The modern financial professional now focuses on combining conventional knowledge with innovative technology. He has proven how to innovate without losing sight of long-term objectives by illustrating that daring and caution coexist.

Bessent's legacy's capacity to turn obstacles into opportunities is among its most motivating features. Whether geopolitical, technical, or financial, he sees no threats from disturbances. Instead, he sees them as sparks of creativity. He aggressively teaches others this viewpoint so they may flourish in an uncertain environment.

Scott Bessent is passing the torch, leaving behind a set of accomplishments and a road map for creativity, inspiration, and leadership. His impact will surely help to mold the next generation of financial innovators, guaranteeing that the sector keeps developing and stretching limits. His legacy concerns what others will create because of him rather than only what he has produced.

Scott Bessent

Scott's Influence On International Market

It is impressive how much Scott Bessent influences foreign markets. A genuine global thinker, he has shown unmatched foresight and action on changes in the linked web of the world economy.

Unquestionably, Bessent's influence on the international financial scene shapes techniques that change how worldwide markets are handled and audacious deals that span continents.

Among his most well-known contributions was made while working for Soros Fund Management, especially during the 1992 currency crisis that shook Europe. Bessent was important in the historic shorting of the British pound. This trade brought billions and revealed flaws in the European Exchange Rate Mechanism.

This action was a profound lesson on the power of knowledge of international monetary policy and its practical effects, not only a financial masterstroke. It also confirmed Bessent as a force that can affect markets and the systems inside which they run.

Bessent's career is evidence of his capacity for a whole-market approach. He envisions a dynamic network of interactions whereby one nation's policy change can shock the markets of another, not only isolated economies.

Scott Bessent

From political upheavals to technological revolutions, this point of view has helped him negotiate complex worldwide events with a precision few others can equal.

Through his work with Key Square Group, Bessent continued impacting global markets by targeting long-term macroeconomic patterns. His company's emphasis on developing nations, especially Asia, showcased a strong awareness of the direction of world growth.

Bessent demonstrated the need to balance audacious vision and thorough analysis by spotting underpriced prospects in areas deemed too dangerous or turbulent.

Bessent's impact is also evident in his attitude toward worldwide risk management. His capacity to guard against geopolitical uncertainty and economic downturns offers a road map for investors navigating a globe growing in unpredictable nature. He has shown that success in foreign markets calls for spotting possibilities and handling the complexity accompanying them.

Bessent's significance goes beyond his trades to include his influence on investor perceptions of the world economy. His observations have guided the financial sector toward a more linked knowledge of markets in which macroeconomic trends, cultural subtleties, and political events influence significantly.

By doing this, he has motivated a generation of investors to see internationally, act strategically,

Scott Bessent

and welcome the always-shifting character of foreign markets.

Scott Bessent's influence on foreign markets serves as a sobering reminder of the power a visionary may have, not only in creating returns but also in changing the global financial scene itself. His ideas, insight, and flexibility have made a lasting impression that guarantees his name will be connected with worldwide market innovation for years.

CONCLUSION

As we close the last chapter on Scott Bessent: The Visionary Investor, one thing stands out: Scott Bessent is a force of nature in the financial environment, not only a guy of numbers and deals. His narrative celebrates audacious ideas, unwavering curiosity, and the unrelenting search for innovation, not only market successes and epic transactions.

Bessent's path from aspirational Wall Street analyst to one of the most revered names in global finance is a masterclass in perseverance and adaptation. He produced the waves of the markets, not merely rode them. With his trademark mix of intellectual rigidity and innovative problem-solving, Bessent changed the definition of global macro investment. He is a game-changer, not merely a participant in the game.

Scott's impact is striking not only in his great successes but also in the humanity behind them. He is a leader who supports education, guides developing talent, and welcomes the beauty of measured risk.

Bessent's approach, think significant, be modest, and always be ready to change, stands out in an industry noted for its savagery. It reminds us that trust, creativity, and a relentless dedication to quality create the most enduring legacies, even in the hectic financial environment.

Scott Bessent's career proves that people who are ready to see the future differently can eventually own it. Being a visionary is about asking the proper questions, perceiving the invisible, and daring to act when others pause and do not have all the answers. His narrative motivates dreamers and investors to welcome the future and produce something remarkable.

We find an energising effect when we distance ourselves from Scott's universe. His path teaches us wisdom in learning from every experience, magic in seeing beyond the apparent, and power in taking risks.

At its core, Scott Bessent's story is about vision, vision to perceive possibilities, grab opportunities, and construct a future brighter than anyone dared imagine, even if it is about cash.

Scott Bessent

Then, Scott Bessent is the visionary, doer, and disruptor. His legacy resides in the brains he inspired and the markets he shaped. Furthermore, the narrative of his influence is still ongoing, even if this book is closed. True visionaries never cease creating; they set the stage for what will come.

Made in the USA
Monee, IL
20 January 2025